You are more powerful than you appear.

If you believe in magic, you will perceive it.

Or do you have a Growth Mindset?

A belief that intellect, skills, and potential can be expanded through strong efforts, good strategies, and assistance from others.

Be more ferocious than your fears.

Your mind believes what you tell it -
so tell it good things!

Tell it you are a Warrior.
Tell it you are Grateful.
Tell it you are Kind.

Make a list of what you admire in other people.
DO THAT.
Make a list of what you dislike in others.
Avoid doing that.

Live your truth.

Choose who you are.

Take mercy on
your Self.
You only have
the knowledge
that you have.

Forgive
your Self for
the mistakes you
made in the past,
and the ones
you will make
in th future.

Play without being self-conscious.

The things that excite you are connected to your purpose.

Feeling lost at times is a part of life.

The most intoxicating thing that exists for a human, is another human.

Love says, "I would live for You."

Sometimes your loved one is not meant to be your always and forever.

Love cannot be found where it doesn't exist.

You can Not have someone who's not ready for you.

Lovers will vanish,
Love will endure.

Your chosen mindset should reflect your hopes, not your fears.

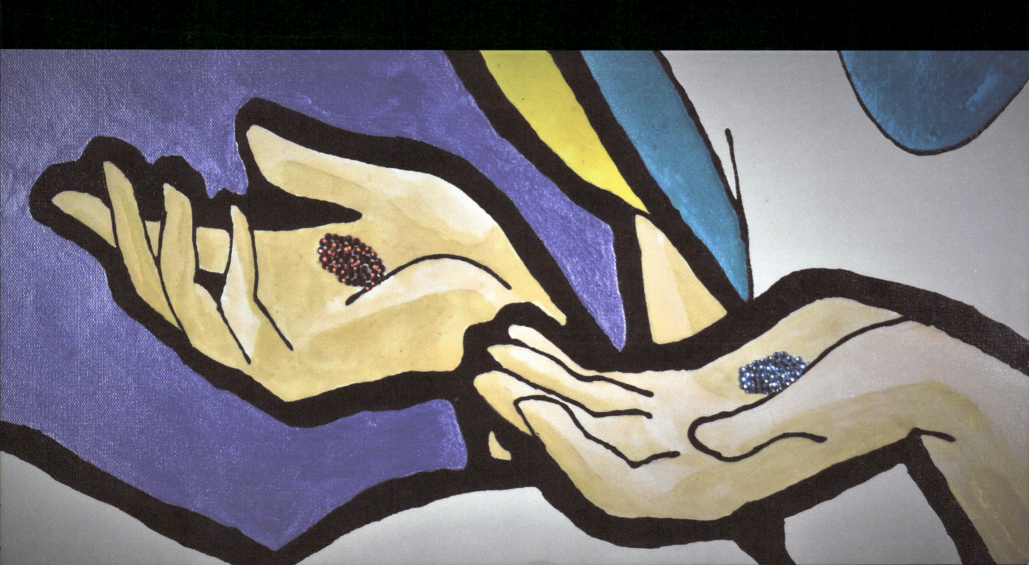

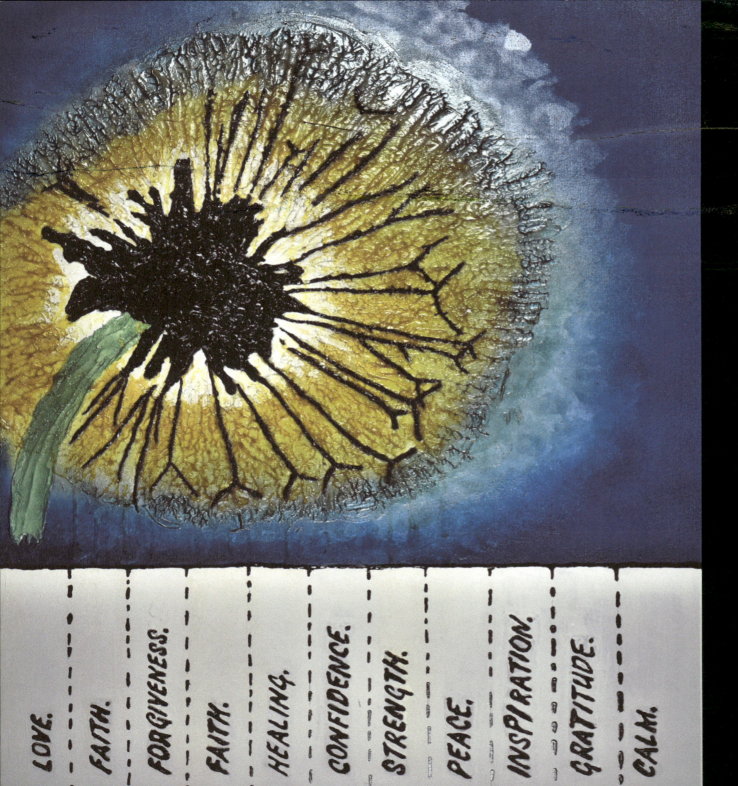

It's easier to navigate if you are always moving forward.

If you can be anything,
be Kind.

Have compassion for your Self.

We are all imperfect.

Happy people choose their inner world.

Unhappy people condemn the outer world.

I am more than Enough.

I am more than Enough.

I am more than Enough.

I am more than Enough.

Every day is a new opportunity to become a better version of yourself.

:(:

Choose Well.

Thank you.

Dee McClure - Jo Ann Jonas - Debra Benton

Tina, Maria, Jerry, Rosa, Kurt, Francie, Sergio, Miguel, Hilda, Avel, Michele, Angelina, Veronika, Marisela, Adriana, Seamus, Mikey, Athena, Daphne, Luna, Michael, Loreen, Jerry, Kyle, Randy, Dennis, Cindy, Marnell, Jimmy, Norma, Ally, Dan, Tracy, Karen, Rick, Debby, Chris, Mick, Sean, Kurt, Antoinette, Don, Jamie, Kevin, Anne, Lane, Doris, Larry, Connie, Doug, Rick, Kathy, Evelyn, Tammy, Barbara, Yolanda, Kevin, Stacy, Angelica, Pam, Kathee, Miles, Lauren, Jesus.

THANK YOU TO ALL THAT PREVIEWED THIS BOOK AT EL CHARRO AVITIA

A special thank you to my hometown Bishop, CA

Art encourages us to imagine and anticipate
a better Self, community, and world.   Tony Avitia

Copyright © 2018 by Tony Avitia

All rights reserved. No part of this publication may be reproduced, distributed, or transmitted in any form or by any means, including photocopying, recording, or other electronic or mechanical methods, without the prior written permission of the publisher, except in the case of brief quotations embodied in critical reviews and certain other noncommercial uses permitted by copyright law. For permission requests, write to Amuzed Art at amuzedart@yahoo.com

Amuzed Art LLC.
4389 S. Carson St.
Carson City, NV. 89701

amuzedart@yahoo.com   www.selfregards.com.com   amuzedart.com

ISBN 9780999697870   Library of congress Control Number:n2018900444

Printed in the USA
CPSIA information can be obtained
at www.ICGtesting.com
LVHW060839101023

760668LV00004B/156